Microwave Cooking

9

The Fifth Vegetarian Cookbook

Wancy Ganst

ISBN-13: 978-1466280588
ISBN-10: 1466280581

E-mail: wancyganst@yahoo.com

INTRODUCTION

RECIPES

DOS

- ✓ Use the cookware and plastic wrap that are labelled as 'Microwave-safe' or 'Microwaveable'.
- ✓ Leave a small corner of the container vented when reheating or cooking food, unless the instruction from recipes indicates that the food should be covered during cooking, but it should still be taken care to prevent steam build up to dangerous levels.
- ✓ Circular or oval containers are recommended as energy absorption occurs evenly around the edges and hence it helps preventing the edges of the food get burn.
- ✓ Arrange the thinner parts of the food toward the center of the microwave oven, as the outside sections of the food are always cook more quickly due to the unevenly heating from microwave oven.

DON'TS

- × Never use any cookware that made by metal, such as aluminum foil, steel, or utensils, or any cookware that is not designed to be used in the microwave oven.
- × Don't operate the oven while there is empty inside.
- × Don't heat water or any liquid beyond the recommended time. Superheating would cause the water or liquid erupts out of the container when moved.
- × Don't heat or cook eggs before those are shelled and the yolks are not pricked, as it can cause the eggs to blow.

- Microwave cooking enhances water-soluble vitamins (eg, vitamin C and thiamine) and minerals retention in vegetables.

- Higher quality of protein is got and vitamins A and E are better retained when food cooked in microwave oven than with conventional method, as less oxidation and browning occurred, although there is only a slightly difference.

- More nutrients can be retained when reheating food quickly in a microwave oven than holding food hot for long periods.

Microwave Time and Wattage Conversion Chart

500W	600W	700W	800W	**850W**	900W	1000W	1200W
00:17	00:14	00:12	00:11	**00:10**	00:09	00:09	00:07
00:34	00:28	00:24	00:22	**00:20**	00:18	00:18	00:14
00:51	00:42	00:36	00:33	**00:30**	00:27	00:27	00:21
01:42	01:24	01:12	01:06	**01:00**	00:54	00:54	00:42
03:24	02:48	02:24	02:12	**02:00**	01:48	01:48	01:24
08:30	07:00	06:00	05:30	**05:00**	04:30	04:30	03:30
10:12	08:24	07:12	06:36	**06:00**	05:24	05:24	04:12
13:36	11:12	09:36	08:48	**08:00**	07:12	07:12	05:36
17:00	14:00	12:00	11:00	**10:00**	09:00	09:00	07:00

The recipes written in this book are used 850-watt microwave oven as standard.

People who decide to be vegetarians can due to different reasons, such as health, religions, cultures, environmental or ethical reasons, etc. Therefore, there are also different types of vegetarians.

- Raw Vegans, who only eat fresh and uncooked fruits, nuts, seeds and vegetables that can be cooked only up to a certain temperature.

- Vegans, who do not eat any animal flesh and its products, such as milk, eggs, honey and yeast. They also do not use the products that are from animals or tested on animals.

- Ovo-Vegetarians, who do not eat any animal flesh and dairy products but they would eat eggs.

- Lacto-Vegetarians, who do not eat any animal flesh and eggs but they would consume dairy products.

- Lacto-Ovo-Vegetarians (or Ovo-Lacto-Vegetarians), who do not eat any animal flesh but they do eat eggs and consume dairy products, such as milk and cheese.

- Fruitarians, who only eat fruits, nuts, seeds and plant matters that can be obtained without harming the plants.

- Buddhist-Vegetarians, who do not eat any animal flesh and its products, and also onion, garlic, scallions, leeks and shallots. Moreover, alcohol is prohibited because it is addictive. And due to the Buddhist precept of ahimsa (non-violence), some of the Buddhist vegetarians even exclude root vegetables, such as potato and carrot, as this can cause the plants to death. However, such diet is only practiced during some special occasions.

- Semi-Vegetarians, who consume not only vegetables. Some of them would eat also fishes, shellfishes and seafood (Pescetarians), poultry (Pollotarians) or both (Pollo-Pescatarians).

Since there is only general vegetarian food introduced in this book, therefore, eggs, milk, cheese, onion, garlic, potato, etc are included in some of the recipes.

Apple, Carrot and Hairy Cucumber Soup

Baby Cobs, Winter Bamboo Shoots and Tomato Soup

Abalone Mushroom, Black Fungus, Carrot, Sweet Corn and Tofu Soup

Green Papaya, Potato, Hairy Cucumber and Egg Tofu Soup

Common Fig, Tangerine Peel, Tofu and Wolfberries Soup

Garlic Chives, Shiitake Mushrooms and Miso Soup

Radish, Shimeji Mushrooms, Red Dates and Wolfberries Soup

Beetroot, Coconut and Mushrooms Soup

Assorted Mushrooms, Red Dates and Wolfberries Soup

Carrot and Hairy Cucumber Soup

Cobs, Winter Bamboo Shoots
and Tomato Soup

Potato, Hairy Cucumber
Soup

Fig, Tangerine Peel,

Garlic Chives, Shiitake Mushrooms
and Miso Soup

Beetroot, Coconut and Mushrooms Soup

Apple, Carrot and Hairy Cucumber Soup

SERVE

1~2

INGREDIENTS

150g Apple (cored & cut into chunks)
200g Carrot (peeled & cut into chunks)
200g Hairy Cucumber (peeled & cut into chunks)
1000ml Water
Salt

METHOD

Prepare a microwave-safe container, put apple, carrot and hairy cucumber in, and pour water in. Cover the container with microwave wrap. Put them in the microwave oven, microwave for 8 minutes (850W) and stay put in the microwave oven for 5 minutes.

Keep them in the microwave oven. Microwave them for 8 minutes (850W) and stay put in the microwave oven for 5 minutes. Repeat this step 3 times.

Still keep them in the microwave oven and microwave for 3 minutes (850W).

Take them out from the microwave oven and remove the microwave wrap. Season with salt. Serve.

Baby Cobs, Winter Bamboo Shoots and Tomato Soup

SERVE

1~2

INGREDIENTS

150g Tomato (cut into chunks)
100g Canned Baby Cobs (rinsed)
100g Canned Winter Bamboo Shoots (rinsed)
1 tsp Oil
500ml Water
Salt

METHOD

Prepare a microwave-safe container, put tomato, baby cobs, winter bamboo shoots, oil and water in. Put them in the microwave oven and microwave for 5 minutes (850W).

Take them out from the microwave oven. Season with salt. Serve.

Abalone Mushroom, Black Fungus, Carrot, Sweet Corn and Tofu Soup

SERVE

1~2

INGREDIENTS

50g Abalone Mushroom (shredded)
30g Dried Black Fungus
50g Carrot (peeled & shredded)
100g Frozen Sweet Corns (rinsed)
100g Tofu (cubed)
2/3 tsp Tapioca Flour
Water
Salt

METHOD

Prepare a normal container, put dried black fungus in, and pour water in until the black fungus is fully covered. Soak black fungus in water until tendered. Drain it off and slice it.

Blend 2/3 teaspoon of tapioca flour well with 1 tablespoon of water. Put 50g of sweet corns in a food processor and blend them into puree.

Prepare a microwave-safe container, put abalone mushrooms, black fungus, carrot, sweet corns, sweet corn puree and tofu in, and pour 800ml of water in. Put them in the microwave oven, microwave for 8 minutes (850W) and stay put in the microwave oven for 4 minutes.

Keep them in the microwave oven. Microwave them for another 8 minutes (850W) and stay put in the microwave oven for 4 minutes.

Take them out from the microwave oven. Add tapioca flour mixture in. Put them back in the microwave oven and microwave for 2 minutes (850W). Take them out from the microwave oven. Season with salt. Serve.

Green Papaya, Potato, Hairy Cucumber and Egg Tofu Soup

SERVE

1~2

INGREDIENTS

150g Green Papaya (peeled & cut into chunks)
150g Hairy Cucumber (peeled & cut into chunks)
100g Potato (peeled & cut into chunks)
100g Egg Tofu (cut into chunks)
1000ml Water
Salt

METHOD

Prepare a microwave-safe container, put green papaya, hairy cucumber, potato and egg tofu in, and pour water in. Cover the container with microwave wrap. Put them in the microwave oven, microwave for 8 minutes (850W) and stay put in the microwave oven for 5 minutes.

Keep them in the microwave oven. Microwave them for 8 minutes (850W) and stay put in the microwave oven for 5 minutes. Repeat this step twice.

Still keep them in the microwave oven and microwave for the last 3 minutes (850W).

Take them out from the microwave oven. Season with salt. Serve.

Common Fig, Tangerine Peel, Tofu and Wolfberries Soup

SERVE

1~2

INGREDIENTS

100g Tofu (cubed)
50g Dried Common Figs (rinsed & cut into halves)
10g Dried Tangerine Peel (rinsed)
2/3 tbsp Dried Wolfberries (rinsed)
800ml Water
Salt

METHOD

Prepare a microwave-safe container, put tofu, common figs, tangerine peel and wolfberries in, and pour water in. Cover the container with microwave wrap. Put them in the microwave oven, microwave for 8 minutes (850W) and stay put in the microwave oven for 4 minutes.

Keep them in the microwave oven. Microwave them for 8 minutes (850W) and stay put in the microwave oven for 4 minutes.

Take them out from the microwave oven and remove the microwave wrap. Season with salt. Put them in the microwave oven and microwave them for 3 minutes (850W) to re-heat.

Take them out from the microwave oven. Stir to mix the soup well. Serve.

Garlic Chives, Shiitake Mushrooms and Miso Soup

SERVE

1~2

INGREDIENTS

150g Garlic Chives (sectioned)
8 Dried Shiitake Mushrooms (rinsed)
2/3 tbsp Japanese Miso
700ml Water

METHOD

Prepare a microwave-safe container, put dried shiitake mushrooms in, and pour water in. Soak shiitake mushrooms in water until all are tendered. Take them out, slice them and put them back in the microwave-safe container.

Cover the container with microwave wrap. Put the container with shiitake mushrooms and water in the microwave oven. Microwave them for 8 minutes (850W) and stay put in the microwave oven for 4 minutes.

Take them out from the microwave oven and open the microwave wrap. Add garlic chives and Japanese miso in. Stir to mix them well with shiitake mushrooms. Cover the container back with microwave wrap. Put them in the microwave oven and microwave for 5 minutes (850W).

Take them out from the microwave oven. Stir to mix the soup well. Serve.

Radish, Shimeji Mushrooms, Red Dates and Wolfberries Soup

SERVE

1~2

INGREDIENTS

200g Chinese Radish (peeled & cut into chunks)
150g Shimeji Mushrooms (rinsed)
10 Dried Red Dates (remove seeds & rinsed)
1/2 tbsp Dried Wolfberries (rinsed)
5g Ginger (shredded)
800ml Water
Salt

METHOD

Prepare a microwave-safe container, put radish, shimeji mushrooms, red dates, wolfberries and ginger in, and pour water in. Cover the container with microwave wrap. Put them in the microwave oven, microwave for 8 minutes (850W) and stay put in the microwave oven for 4 minutes.

Keep them in the microwave oven, microwave for 8 minutes (850W) and stay put in the microwave oven for 4 minutes. Repeat this step 3 times.

Still keep them in the microwave oven. Microwave them for the last 3 minutes (850W).

Take them out from the microwave oven. Season with salt. Serve.

Beetroot, Coconut and Mushrooms Soup

SERVE

1~2

INGREDIENTS

150g Canned Mushroom Slices

100g Canned Beetroots

400ml Water

100ml Coconut Milk

Salt

METHOD

Put beetroots and water in a food processor and blend them well.

Prepare a microwave-safe container, pour the beetroot mixture in, and add mushroom slices in. Put them in the microwave oven and microwave for 5 minutes (850W).

Take them out from the microwave oven. Add coconut milk in. Put them in the microwave oven and microwave for 1 minute 30 seconds (850W).

Take them out from the microwave oven. Season with salt and stir to mix the soup well. Serve.

Assorted Mushrooms, Red Dates and Wolfberries Soup

SERVE

1~2

INGREDIENTS

30g Dried Jersey Cow Mushrooms (rinsed)
30g True Red Brittlegills (Russula vinosa, rinsed)
30g Dried Shiitake Mushrooms (rinsed)
30g Dried Black Fungus (rinsed)
30g Canned Bailing Mushroom (rinsed)
5~6 Dried Red Dates (rinsed, seeded & sliced)
1 tsp Dried Wolfberries (rinsed)
800ml Water
Salt

METHOD

Prepare a microwave-safe container, put all the dried mushrooms in, and pour water in. Soak the mushrooms in water until all are tendered. Take the mushrooms out, cut them into chunks and put them back in the container.

Add bailing mushroom, red dates and wolfberries in. Cover the container with microwave wrap. Put them in the microwave oven, microwave for 5 minutes (850W) and stay put in the microwave oven for 4 minutes.

Keep them in the microwave oven. Microwave for another 5 minutes (850W) and stay put in the microwave oven for 4 minutes. Then microwave again for the last 5 minutes (850W).

Take them out from the microwave oven. Season with salt. Serve.

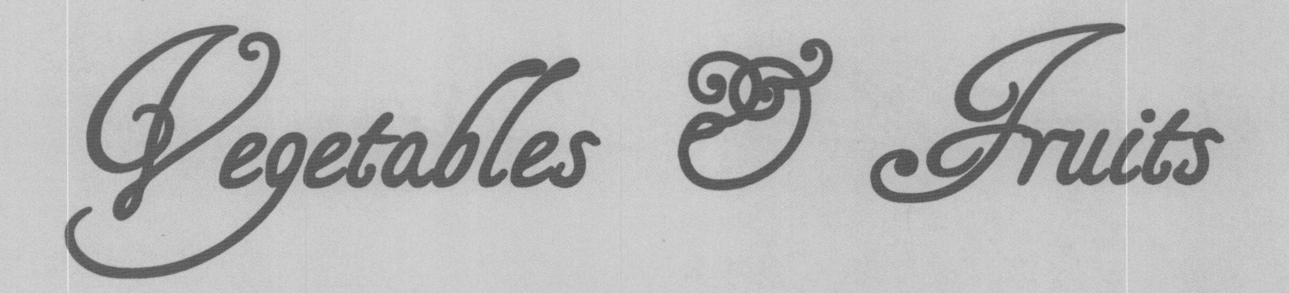

Broccoli Stems, Potato and Tofu Pancake

Sour and Spicy Green Papaya, Chayote, Onion Salad

Sweet Potato Leaves and Potato Cakes

Tofu and Sesame Rolls with Salted Lemon Sauce

Steamed Eggplant in Cucumber and Coriander Sauce

Gingery Coca-Cola Carrot and King Trumpet Mushroom

Deep-Fried Gluten in Lemon and Pineapple Sauce

Peppery Bitter Melon and King Trumpet Mushroom

Simmered Eggplant, Onion and Bell Pepper in Cashew Sauce

Stir-Fried Chickpeas, Bell Pepper and Garlic Chives

Stir-Fried Eggplant, Squash and Lychees

Simmered Mixed Mushrooms with Common Figs

Stir-Fried Five-Spice-Flavoured Cabbage and Deep-Fried Gluten

Stir-Fried Garlic Chives and Bell Peppers

Stir-Fried Eggplant and Potato in Black Pepper Sauce

Stir-Fried Chilli Beans and Bell Peppers in Strawberry Sauce

Stir-Fried Bitter Melon and Winter Bamboo Shoots

Stir-Fried Potato and Carrot in Lemon Sauce

Stir-Fried Potato, Green Papaya and Green Chilli Pepper

Stir-Fried Long White Beans and Sweet Corns in Chinese Black Bean Sauce

Stir-Fried Onion and Sweet Potato in Black Pepper Sauce

Stir-Fried Cucumber and Shimeji Mushrooms in Peanut Sauce

Stir-Fried Bitter Melon, Carrot and Takuan

Stir-Fried Abalone Mushrooms in Tomato Sauce

Stir-Fried Potato and Kiwi Fruit

Stir-Fried Carrot and Black Fungus in Gingery Soy Sauce

Stir-Fried Potato, Mushrooms and Raisins

Stir-Fried Green Papaya, Kimchi and Mushrooms

Stir-Fried Squash and Bitter Melon

Stir-Fried Bitter Melon, Baby Cobs and Bailing Mushroom

Stir-Fried Sweet Potato in Three-Cups Sauce

Stems, Potato and

Spicy Green Papaya,
Salad

Tofu and Sesame Rolls
Salted Lemon Sauce

Gingery
King Trumpet Mushroom

Deep-Fried Gluten
in Lemon and Pineapple Sauce

Bitter
and King Trumpet Mushroom

Simmered Eggplant, Onion and Bell Pepper in Cashew Sauce

Stir-Fried Chickpeas, Bell Pepper and Garlic Chives

Stir-Fried Garlic Chives and Bell Peppers

Stir-Fried Chilli Beans and Bell Peppers in Strawberry Sauce

Stir-Fried Bitter Melon and Winter Bamboo Shoots

Stir-Fried Potato, Green Papaya and Green Chilli Pepper

Stir-Fried Bitter Melon, Carrot and Takuan

Stir-Fried Abalone Mushrooms in Tomato Sauce

Stir-Fried Potato, Mushrooms and Raisins

Stir-Fried Green Papaya, Kimchi and Mushrooms

Stir-Fried Squash and Bitter Melon

Stir-Fried Bitter Melon, Baby Cobs [illegible] Mushroom

Broccoli Stems, Potato and Tofu Pancake

SERVE

1~2

INGREDIENTS

100g Broccoli Stems
100g Potato (peeled)
100g Soy Slurry
A pinch of Salt
Water

METHOD

Prepare a microwave-safe container, put potato in, and pour water in until 1/3 of potato is covered. Put them in the microwave oven and microwave for 8 minutes (850W).

Take them out from the microwave oven. Drain off and mash the potato.

Put broccoli stems, soy slurry and salt in a food processor and blend them well. Pour the mixture in the container with potato mash and mix them well.

Prepare a baking paper, spread the mixture on. Put them in the microwave oven and microwave for 6 minutes (850W).

Take the pancake out from the microwave oven. Cool it in room temperature for a while. Cut it into several pieces. Serve with any dipping sauce preferred.

TIPS & NOTES

- Soya slurry is the grounded soya beans, which is the side product after making soya milk. It can be substituted by tofu.
- The dipping sauce I made to serve with the pancakes is chilli mayonnaise, which just simply blend Korean red chilli paste and Japanese mayonnaise together.

Sour and Spicy Green Papaya, Chayote, Onion Salad

SERVE

1~2

INGREDIENTS

150g Green Papaya (peeled & cut into chunks)
150g Chayote (peeled & cut into chunks)
150g Onion (peeled & cut into chunks)
100g Canned Pineapple Tidbits
2/3 tbsp Olive Oil
1 tsp Chopped Garlic

SOUR AND SPICY SAUCE

100g Tomato (sliced)
1 tbsp Water
1/2 tbsp Red Chilli Sauce
1/2 tbsp Lemon Juice
1 tsp Sugar
1/3 tsp Salt

METHOD

Put tomato in a food processor and blend it into juice.

Prepare a microwave-safe container, put onion, chopped garlic and olive oil in, and mix them well. Put them in the microwave oven and microwave for 1 minute 30 seconds (850W).

Take them out from the microwave oven. Add green papaya and chayote in. Stir to mix them well with onion. Put them in the microwave oven and microwave for 2 minutes (850W).

Take them out from the microwave oven. Stir again to mix the ingredients well. Let them cool down in room temperature.

Prepare another microwave-safe container, put tomato juice, water, red chilli sauce, sugar and salt in. Stir to mix them well. Put them in the microwave oven and microwave for 1 minute 30 seconds (850W).

Take them out from the microwave oven. Add lemon juice in, and stir to mix the sauce well. Spoon the sauce over green papaya, chayote and onion. Mix them well before serving.

Sweet Potato Leaves and Potato Cakes

MAKE

8 Cakes

INGREDIENTS

250g Potato (peeled)
150g Sweet Potato Leaves (chopped & keep 8 leaves)
1/2 tbsp Oil
1/3 tsp Salt
Water

METHOD

Prepare a microwave-safe container, put potato in, and pour water in until 1/3 of potato is covered. Put them in the microwave oven and microwave for 7 minutes (850W).

Take the potato out from the microwave oven. Drain it off and put it in a normal container.

Use the same microwave-safe container, put sweet potato leaves (except the 8 leaves that kept to be used later) and oil in, and mix them well. Put them in the microwave oven and microwave for 2 minutes (850W).

Take them out from the microwave oven. Put potato and salt in. Mash potato and mix it well with sweet potato leaves. Divide the mixture into 8 portions.

Flatten the 8 sweet potato leaves, put the mixtures on and wrap them respectively.

Prepare another microwave-safe container, put the packages in. Put them in the microwave oven and microwave for 2 minutes (850W).

Take them out from the microwave oven and serve.

Tofu and Sesame Rolls with Salted Lemon Sauce

SERVE

1~2

INGREDIENTS

150g Tofu
2 Japanese Nori (Japanese Edible Seaweed)
1/3 Salted Lemon (sliced)
1 tbsp White Sesames
1 tbsp Tapioca Flour
1 tsp Sugar
1/2 tsp Salt
Water

METHOD

Prepare a microwave-safe container, put tofu and salt in, and pour water in until the tofu is covered. Put them in the microwave oven and microwave for 5 minutes (850W).

Take them out from the microwave oven. Drain the tofu off and crush it. Add white sesames and tapioca flour in, and mix them well with tofu.

Flatten Japanese nori, put the tofu mixture on and roll them up.

Prepare another microwave-safe container, put tofu and sesame rolls in. Then add salted lemon, sugar and 100ml of water in. Put them in the microwave oven and microwave for 2 minutes 30 seconds (850W).

Take them out from the microwave oven. Section the tofu and sesame rolls and spoon the salted lemon sauce over them. Serve.

in Cucumber and Coriander Sauce

SERVE

1~2

INGREDIENTS

300g Eggplant (peeled & sliced)
100g Cucumber (cut into chunks)
50g Coriander (sectioned)
1/3 tbsp Oil
200ml Water
Salt

METHOD

Put cucumber, coriander, water and salt in a food processor and blend them well.

Prepare a microwave-safe container, put eggplant, oil and the sauce in. Put them in the microwave oven and microwave for 5 minutes (850W).

Take them out from the microwave oven. Spoon the sauce over the eggplant. Serve.

Gingery Coca-Cola Carrot and King Trumpet Mushroom

SERVE

1~2

INGREDIENTS

250g Carrot (peeled & sliced)

250g King Trumpet Mushroom (sliced)

3/4 tbsp Oil

1/2 tbsp Chopped Ginger

1/3 tsp Salt

250ml Coke

METHOD

Prepare a microwave-safe container, put carrot, chopped ginger and oil in, and mix them well. Put them in the microwave oven and microwave for 2 minutes (850W).

Take them out from the microwave oven. Add king trumpet mushroom and salt in, and pour coke in. Stir to mix all ingredients well. Put them in the microwave oven and microwave for 5 minutes (850W).

Take them out from the microwave oven. Stir one more time. Serve.

Deep-Fried Gluten in Lemon and Pineapple Sauce

SERVE

1~2

INGREDIENTS

200g Deep-Fried Gluten (rinsed & cut into chunks)
150g Canned Pineapple Tidbits
1 tbsp Sugar
1/2 tsp Tapioca Flour
50ml Lemon Juice
50ml Water
A pinch of Salt

METHOD

Prepare a microwave-safe container, put deep-fried gluten in. Put them in the microwave oven and microwave for 3 minutes (850W). Take them out from the microwave oven.

Prepare another microwave-safe container, put sugar, tapioca flour, lemon juice, water and salt in. Stir to mix them well. Put them in the microwave oven and microwave for 2 minutes (850W).

Take them out from the microwave oven. Add deep-fried gluten and pineapple in. Stir to mix them well with the sauce. Put them in the microwave oven and microwave for 1 minute (850W).

Take them out from the microwave oven. Stir once more and serve.

Peppery Bitter Melon and King Trumpet Mushroom

SERVE

1~2

INGREDIENTS

200g Bitter Melon (remove seeds & cut into chunks)
250g King Trumpet Mushroom (cut into chunks)
3/4 tbsp Oil
1/2 tbsp Black Pepper
1 tsp Chopped Garlic
1/2 tsp White Pepper
Salt

METHOD

Prepare a microwave-safe container, put king trumpet mushroom, oil, black pepper, white pepper and chopped garlic in, and mix them well. Put them in the microwave oven and microwave for 3 minutes (850W).

Take them out from the microwave oven. Add bitter melon in. Stir to mix all ingredients well. Put them in the microwave oven and microwave for 3 minutes (850W).

Take them out from the microwave oven. Season with salt and stir one more time. Serve.

Simmered Eggplant, Onion and Bell Pepper in Cashew Sauce

SERVE

1~2

INGREDIENTS

200g Eggplant (cubed)
1/4 Medium-Sized Onion (peeled & cut into chunks)
1/4 Red Bell Pepper (remove seeds & cut into chunks)
1 tbsp Oil

CASHEW SAUCE

50g Roasted Cashew Nuts
1/3 tsp Salt
250ml Water

METHOD

Put all ingredients of cashew sauce in a food processor and blend them well.

Prepare a microwave-safe container, put onion and oil in, and mix them well. Put them in the microwave oven and microwave for 2 minutes (850W).

Take them out from the microwave oven. Add eggplant, red bell pepper and cashew sauce in. Stir to mix all ingredients well. Put them in the microwave oven and microwave for 4 minutes (850W).

Take them out from the microwave oven. Stir once more and serve.

Stir-Fried Chickpeas, Bell Pepper and Garlic Chives

SERVE

1~2

INGREDIENTS

150g Garlic Chives (sectioned)
150g Canned Chickpeas (rinsed)
150g Red Bell Pepper (remove seeds & diced)
2/3 tbsp Oil
1/2 tbsp Light Soy Sauce
1/2 tbsp Ginger Juice
1/3 tsp Sugar

METHOD

Prepare a microwave-safe container, put garlic chives and oil in, and mix them well. Put them in the microwave oven and microwave for 2 minutes (850W).

Take them out from the microwave oven. Add all other ingredients in. Stir to mix them well with garlic chives. Put them in the microwave oven and microwave for another 2 minutes (850W).

Take them out from the microwave oven. Stir one more time and serve.

Stir-Fried Eggplant, Squash and Lychees

SERVE

1~2

INGREDIENTS

250g Eggplant (peeled & cut into chunks)
150g Squash (peeled, remove seeds & cut into chunks)
100g Lychees (peeled & remove seeds)
1 tbsp Oil
1 tbsp Water
A pinch of Salt

METHOD

Prepare a microwave-safe container, put eggplant and oil in, and mix them well. Put them in the microwave oven and microwave for 2 minutes (850W).

Take them out from the microwave oven. Add squash and water in, and mix them well with eggplant. Put them in the microwave oven and microwave for 2 minutes (850W).

Take them out from the microwave oven. Add lychees and salt in. Stir to mix all ingredients well. Put them in the microwave oven and microwave for 30 seconds (850W).

Take them out from the microwave oven. Stir one more time. Serve.

Simmered Mixed Mushrooms with Common Figs

SERVE

1~2

INGREDIENTS

80g Dried Jersey Cow Mushrooms (rinsed)
80g Dried Shiitake Mushrooms (rinsed)
10 Dried Common Figs (cut into halves)
1 tbsp Light Soy Sauce
2/3 tbsp Ginger Juice
1 tsp Sugar
200ml Water
Pepper

METHOD

Prepare a microwave-safe container, put all the dried mushrooms in, and pour water in. Soak the mushrooms in water until all are tendered. Take the mushrooms out, cut them into chunks and put them back in the container. Add common figs in. Cover the container with microwave wrap. Put them in the microwave oven and microwave for 5 minutes (850W).

Take them out from the microwave oven and open the microwave wrap. Add light soy sauce, ginger juice and sugar in. Stir to mix them well with mushrooms and figs. Cover the container back with microwave wrap. Put them in the microwave oven and microwave for 3 minutes (850W).

Take them out from the microwave oven and remove the microwave oven. Season with pepper and stir one more time. Serve.

Stir-Fried Five-Spice-Flavoured Cabbage and Deep-Fried Gluten

SERVE

1~2

INGREDIENTS

300g Cabbage (sliced)
150g Deep-Fried Gluten (rinsed & shredded)
1 tbsp Chinese Rice Wine
1 tbsp Water
2/3 tbsp Light Soy Sauce
1 tsp Sugar
1/3 tsp Five-Spice Powder

METHOD

Prepare a microwave-safe container, put deep-fried gluten in. Put them in the microwave oven and microwave for 2 minutes 30 seconds (850W).

Take them out from the microwave oven. Add light soy sauce, Chinese rice wine, water, sugar and five-spice powder in, and mix them well with gluten. Then add cabbage on top. Put them in the microwave oven and microwave for 2 minutes 30 seconds (850W).

Take them out from the microwave oven. Stir to mix all ingredients well. Serve.

TIPS & NOTES

- The five-spice powder used in this recipe is mixed with ground tangerine peels, cumin, cinnamon barks, Sichuan pepper and star anise.

Stir-Fried Garlic Chives and Bell Peppers

SERVE

1~2

INGREDIENTS

150g Garlic Chives (sectioned)
1/2 Red Bell Pepper (remove seeds & sliced)
1/2 Yellow Bell Pepper (remove seeds & sliced)
2/3 tbsp Oil
Salt

METHOD

Prepare a microwave-safe container, put garlic chives and oil in, and mix them well. Put them in the microwave oven and microwave for 2 minutes (850W).

Take them out from the microwave oven. Add bell peppers in. Stir to mix them well with garlic chives. Put them in the microwave oven and microwave for 2 minutes (850W).

Take them out from the microwave oven. Season with salt and stir to mix all ingredients well. Serve.

Stir-Fried Eggplant and Potato in Black Pepper Sauce

SERVE

1~2

INGREDIENTS

250g Eggplant (cut into chunks)
250g Potato (peeled & cut into chunks)
1.5 tbsp Oil

BLACK PEPPER SAUCE

3 tbsp Black Coffee
1.5 tbsp Shaoxing Wine
3/4 tbsp Light Soy Sauce
1/2 tbsp Black Pepper
1 tsp Sugar
1/2 tsp White Pepper

METHOD

Prepare a microwave-safe container, put eggplant, oil and black pepper in, and mix them well. Put them in the microwave oven and microwave for 1 minute (850W).

Take them out from the microwave oven. Add potato and all other ingredients of black pepper sauce in. Stir to mix them well. Put them in the microwave oven and microwave for 4 minutes (850W).

Take them out from the microwave oven. Stir one more time. Serve.

Stir-Fried Chilli Beans and Bell Peppers in Strawberry Sauce

SERVE

1~2

INGREDIENTS

150g Canned Chilli Beans (including pinto, kidney and black beans, rinsed)
1/2 Red Bell Pepper (remove seeds & diced)
1/2 Yellow Bell Pepper (remove seeds & diced)
2/3 tbsp Oil
1/2 tbsp Chopped Garlic
1 tsp Strawberry Jam
1/4 tsp Salt

METHOD

Prepare a microwave-safe container, put bell peppers, oil and chopped garlic in, and mix them well. Put them in the microwave oven and microwave for 1 minute 30 seconds (850W).

Take them out from the microwave oven. Add chilli beans, strawberry jam and salt in. Stir to mix all ingredients well. Put them in the microwave oven and microwave for 2 minutes (850W).

Take them out from the microwave oven. Stir one more time. Serve.

Stir-Fried Bitter Melon and Winter Bamboo Shoots

SERVE

1~2

INGREDIENTS

200g Bitter Melon (remove seeds & sliced)
200g Canned Winter Bamboo Shoots (rinsed & sliced)
2/3 tbsp Oil
Salt

METHOD

Prepare a microwave-safe container, put bitter melon, winter bamboo shoots and oil in, and mix them well. Put them in the microwave oven and microwave for 3 minutes (850W).

Take them out from the microwave oven. Season with salt. Put them in the microwave oven and microwave for 1 minute (850W).

Take them out from the microwave oven. Stir once more and serve.

Stir-Fried Potato and Carrot in Lemon Sauce

SERVE

1~2

INGREDIENTS

200g Potato (peeled & cut into chunks)
200g Carrot (peeled & cut into chunks)
3 tbsp Water
1 tbsp Oil
1 tbsp Lemon Juice
1 tsp Sugar
1/4 tsp Salt

METHOD

Prepare a microwave-safe container, put potato, carrot and oil in, and mix them well. Put them in the microwave oven and microwave for 3 minutes (850W).

Take them out from the microwave oven. Add water, lemon juice, sugar and salt in, and mix them well with potato and carrot. Put them in the microwave oven and microwave for 3 minutes (850W).

Take them out from the microwave oven. Stir to mix all ingredients well. Serve.

Stir-Fried Potato, Green Papaya and Green Chilli Pepper

SERVE

1~2

INGREDIENTS

200g Potato (peeled & shredded)
150g Green Papaya (peeled & shredded)
1 Green Chilli Pepper (remove seeds & sliced)
2/3 tbsp Oil
1/4 tsp Salt

METHOD

Prepare a microwave-safe container, put potato, green chilli pepper and oil in, and mix them well. Put them in the microwave oven and microwave for 3 minutes (850W).

Take them out from the microwave oven. Add green papaya and salt in. Stir to mix all ingredients well. Put them in the microwave oven and microwave for 2 minutes (850W).

Take them out from the microwave oven. Stir once more and serve.

Stir-Fried Long White Beans and Sweet Corns in Chinese Black Bean Sauce

SERVE

1~2

INGREDIENTS

250g Long White Beans (sectioned)
100g Frozen Sweet Corns (rinsed)
2 tbsp Water

BLACK BEAN SAUCE

2 tbsp Water
1 tbsp Oil
1 tbsp Light Soy Sauce
2 tsp Chinese Fermented Black Beans (rinsed & crushed)
3/4 tsp Sugar
1/2 tsp Chopped Garlic

METHOD

Prepare a microwave-safe container, put all ingredients of black bean sauce in, and mix them well. Put them in the microwave oven and microwave for 30 seconds (850W).

Take them out from the microwave oven. Add long white beans, sweet corns and water in. Stir to mix all ingredients well. Put them in the microwave oven and microwave for 4 minutes 30 seconds (850W).

Take them out from the microwave oven. Stir one more time. Serve.

Stir-Fried Onion and Sweet Potato in Black Pepper Sauce

SERVE

1~2

INGREDIENTS

250g Sweet Potato (peeled & cut into chunks)
1/2 Medium-Sized Onion (peeled & cut into chunks)
3/4 tbsp Oil
1 tsp Chopped Garlic

BLACK PEPPER SAUCE

3 tbsp Black Coffee
1.5 tbsp Shaoxing Wine
3/4 tbsp Light Soy Sauce
1/2 tbsp Black Pepper
1 tsp Sugar
1/2 tsp White Pepper

METHOD

Prepare a microwave-safe container, put onion, garlic, oil and black pepper in, and mix them well. Put them in the microwave oven and microwave for 2 minutes (850W).

Take them out from the microwave oven. Add sweet potato and all other ingredients of black pepper sauce in. Stir to mix them well with onion. Put them in the microwave oven and microwave for 5 minutes (850W).

Take them out from the microwave oven. Stir one more time. Serve.

Stir-Fried Cucumber and Shimeji Mushrooms in Peanut Sauce

SERVE

1~2

INGREDIENTS

300g Cucumber (peeled & cut into chunks)
100g Shimeji Mushrooms
1 tbsp Oil
2 tbsp Peanut Butter
1/2 tbsp Light Soy Sauce

METHOD

Prepare a microwave-safe container, put cucumber, shimeji mushrooms and oil in, and mix them well. Put them in the microwave oven and microwave for 4 minutes (850W).

Take them out from the microwave oven. Add peanut butter and light soy sauce in. Stir to mix all ingredients well. Put them in the microwave oven and microwave for 2 minutes (850W).

Take them out from the microwave oven. Stir once more and serve.

Stir-Fried Bitter Melon, Carrot and Takuan

SERVE

1~2

INGREDIENTS

150g Bitter Melon (remove seeds & sliced)
150g Carrot (peeled & sliced)
100g Takuan (Japanese Pickled Radish, sliced)
2/3 tbsp Oil
1 tsp Sugar
1/4 tsp Salt

METHOD

Prepare a microwave-safe container, put carrot and oil in, and mix them well. Put them in the microwave oven and microwave for 2 minutes (850W).

Take them out from the microwave oven. Add bitter melon, tukuan, sugar and salt in, and stir to mix them well with carrot. Put them in the microwave oven and microwave for 3 minutes (850W).

Take them out from the microwave oven. Stir one more time and serve.

TIPS & NOTES

- Takuan is also called 'takuwan or 'takuan-zuke' in Japan and known as 'danmuji' in Korea. That is one of the popular traditional Japanese pickles.

Stir-Fried Abalone Mushrooms in Tomato Sauce

SERVE

1~2

INGREDIENTS

150g Abalone Mushrooms (cut into chunks)
75g Chopped Pickled Mustard Greens
1 Medium-Sized Tomato
1 tbsp Oil
Salt
Pepper

METHOD

Cut 3/4 of tomato into chunks and dice 1/4 of tomato. Put the tomato chunks in a food processor and blend them into juice.

Prepare a microwave-safe container, put tomato juice and 1/2 tablespoon of oil in, and mix them well. Put them in the microwave oven and microwave for 3 minutes (850W).

Take the sauce out from the microwave oven. Stir to mix the sauce well.

Prepare another microwave-safe container, put abalone mushrooms, pickled mustard greens, 1/2 tablespoon of oil, a pinch of salt and pepper in, and mix them well. Put them in the microwave oven and microwave for 3 minutes 30 seconds (850W).

Take them out from the microwave oven. Put abalone mushrooms and pickled mustard greens over the tomato sauce in another container. Serve.

Stir-Fried Potato and Kiwi Fruit

SERVE

1~2

INGREDIENTS

250g Potato (peeled & cut into chunks)
150g Kiwi Fruit (peeled & cut into chunks)
2/3 tbsp Oil
1/2 tsp Sugar
A pinch of Salt

METHOD

Prepare a microwave-safe container, put potato and oil in, and mix them well. Put them in the microwave oven and microwave for 4 minutes 30 seconds (850W).

Take them out from the microwave oven. Add kiwi fruit, sugar and salt in. Stir to mix them well with potato. Put them in the microwave oven and microwave for 20 seconds (850W).

Take them out from the microwave oven. Stir gently one more time. Serve.

Stir-Fried Carrot and Black Fungus in Gingery Soy Sauce

SERVE

1~2

INGREDIENTS

200g Carrot (peeled & sliced)
60g Dried Black Fungus
1 tbsp Ginger Beer
2/3 tbsp Oil
1/2 tbsp Light Soy Sauce
Water

METHOD

Prepare a normal container, put dried black fungus in, and pour water in. Soak black fungus in water until tendered. Then drain it off and slice it.

Prepare a microwave-safe container, put carrot and oil in, and mix them well. Put them in the microwave oven and microwave for 2 minutes (850W).

Take them out from the microwave oven. Add black fungus, ginger beer, light soy sauce and 1.5 tablespoon of water in. Stir to mix all ingredients well. Put them in the microwave oven and microwave for 5 minutes (850W).

Take them out from the microwave oven. Stir one more time. Serve.

Stir-Fried Potato, Mushrooms and Raisins

SERVE

1~2

INGREDIENTS

200g Potato (peeled & cut into chunks)

150g Canned Sliced Mushrooms (rinsed)

2/3 tbsp Oil

Raisins

Salt

METHOD

Prepare a microwave-safe container, put potato and oil in, and mix them well. Put them in the microwave oven and microwave for 5 minutes (850W).

Take them out from the microwave oven. Add mushrooms in, and mix them well with potato. Put them in the microwave oven and microwave for 2 minutes (850W).

Take them out from the microwave oven. Add raisins in, and season with salt. Stir all ingredients to mix them well. Serve.

Stir-Fried Green Papaya, Kimchi and Mushrooms

SERVE

1~2

INGREDIENTS

150g Green Papaya (peeled & sliced)
150g Korean Kimchi
150g Canned Sliced Mushrooms (rinsed)
2 cloves Garlic (sliced)
3 tbsp Water
2/3 tbsp Oil
1/2 tsp Sugar

METHOD

Prepare a microwave-safe container, put Korean kimchi, garlic, 1 tablespoon of water, oil and sugar in, and mix them well. Put them in the microwave oven and microwave for 1 minute 30 seconds (850W).

Take them out from the microwave oven. Add green papaya, mushrooms and another 2 tablespoons of water in. Stir to mix all ingredients well. Put them in the microwave oven and microwave for 5 minutes (850W).

Take them out from the microwave oven. Stir one more time. Serve.

Stir-Fried Squash and Bitter Melon

SERVE

1~2

INGREDIENTS

250g Squash (peeled, remove seeds & cut into chunks)
250g Bitter Melon (remove seeds & cut into chunks)
3/4 tbsp Oil
Salt

METHOD

Prepare a microwave-safe container, put squash, bitter melon and oil in, and mix them well. Put them in the microwave oven and microwave for 4 minutes (850W).

Take them out from the microwave oven. Season with salt. Serve.

Stir-Fried Bitter Melon, Baby Cobs and Bailing Mushroom

SERVE

1~2

INGREDIENTS

150g Bitter Melon (remove seeds & cut into chunks)
150g Baby Cobs (sliced)
100g Canned Bailing Mushroom (cut into chunks)
2/3 tbsp Oil
Salt

METHOD

Prepare a microwave-safe container, put bailing mushroom and oil in, and mix them well. Cover the container with microwave wrap. Put them in the microwave oven and microwave for 1 minute 30 seconds (850W).

Take them out from the microwave oven and remove the microwave wrap. Add bitter melon and baby cobs in, and mix them well with bailing mushroom. Put them in the microwave oven and microwave for 3 minutes (850W).

Take them out from the microwave oven. Season with salt. Serve.

Stir-Fried Sweet Potato in Three-Cups Sauce

SERVE

1~2

INGREDIENTS

250g Orange Sweet Potato (peeled & cut into chunks)
2 Dried Red Dates (rinsed, remove seeds & sliced)
3 Ginger Slices
2 cloves Garlic (crushed)
50g Fresh Basil
3/4 tbsp Oil
1 tsp Brown Rock Sugar
1 tsp Black Vinegar

THREE-CUPS SAUCE

1.5 tbsp Sesame Oil
1.5 tbsp Light Soy Sauce
1.5 tbsp Chinese Rice Wine

METHOD

Prepare a microwave-safe container, put ginger slices, garlic and sesame oil in, and mix them well. Put them in the microwave oven and microwave for 2 minutes (850W).

Take them out from the microwave oven. Add sweet potato, red dates, light soy sauce, Chinese rice wine, brown rock sugar and oil in, and mix them well with ginger and garlic. Put them in the microwave oven and microwave for 3 minutes 30 seconds (850W).

Take them out from the microwave oven. Add basil in. Stir to mix the ingredients well. Put them in the microwave oven and microwave for 30 seconds (850W).

Take them out from the microwave oven. Add black vinegar in. Stir one more time. Serve.

TIPS & NOTES

- Three-Cups means one cup of soy sauce, one cup of rice wine and one cup of sesame oil. It is a famous traditional Taiwanese cuisine. Ginger, garlic, sugar and basil are also added in the recipe.

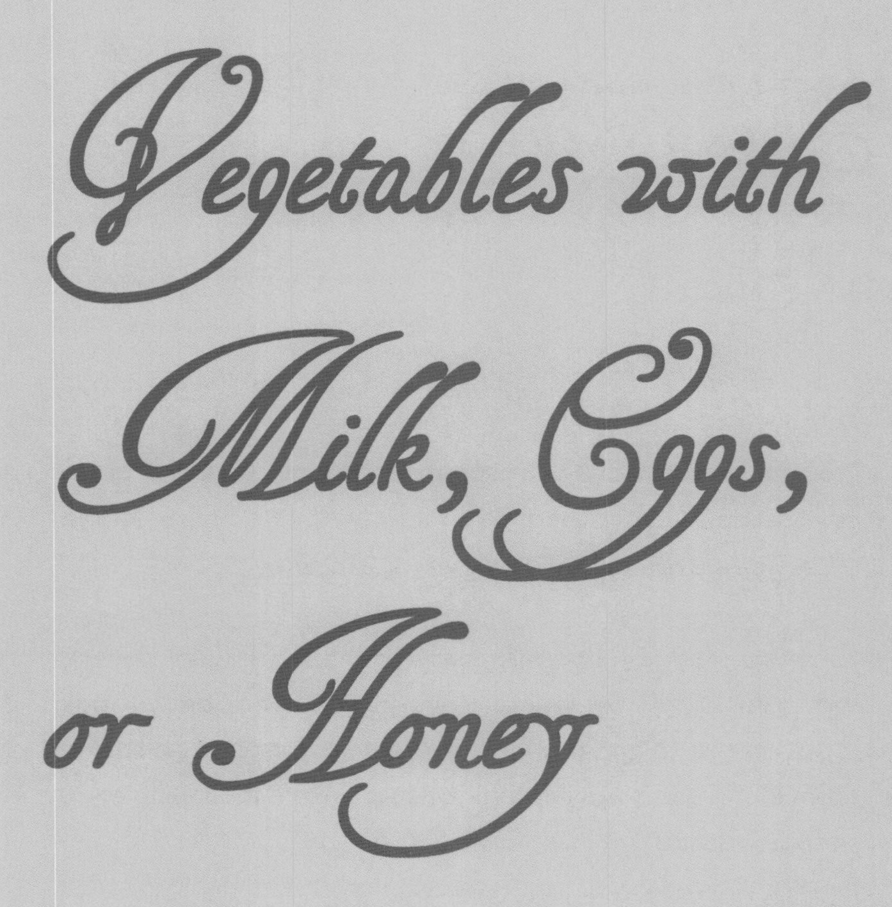

Green Onion and Egg Rolls

Satay Deep-Fried Gluten

Deep-Fried Gluten with Homemade Pandan Kaya

Stewed King Trumpet Mushroom, Winter Melon and Radish

Curried Green Chilli Peppers, Mushrooms and Salted Duck Egg Yolk

Simmered Cabbage, Carrot and Potato in Coconut Milk and Fermented Bean Curd Sauce

Stir-Fried Carrot, Deep-Fried Gluten and Chayote in Peanut-Satay Sauce

Stir-Fried Chickpeas, Pineapple and Green Chilli Peppers in Honey Sauce

Satay Sweet Potato, Onion and Shimeji Mushrooms

Curried Apple, Sweet Potato and Potato

Stir-Fried Hairy Cucumber and Eggs

Satay Bitter Melon and Onion

Potato and Sweet Potato in Portuguese Sauce

Eggplant and Green Onion Omelette

Vegetarian White Sausages

Homemade Vegetable Balls

Simmered Vegetable Balls, Winter Bamboo Shoots and Zucchini in Five-Spice-Flavour

Stir-Fried Vegetable Balls and Broccoli Flowerets

Green Onion and Egg Rolls

Satay Deep-Fried Gluten

[illegible]-Fried Gluten
[illegible] Pandan Kaya

Stewed King Trumpet Mushroom,
Winter Melon and Radish

Curried Green Chilli Peppers, Mushrooms
and Salted Duck Egg Yolk

[illegible]ered Cabbage, Carrot and Potato
[illegible]nut Milk and Fermented Bean Curd Sauce

Stir-Fried Carrot, Deep-Fried Gluten and Chayote in Peanut-Satay Sauce

Stir-Fried Chickpeas, Pineapple and Green Chilli Peppers in Honey Sauce

Curried Apple, Sweet Potato and Potato

Stir-Fried Hairy Cucumber and Eggs

Potato and Sweet Potato in Portuguese Sauce

Vegetarian White Sausages

SERVE

1~2

INGREDIENTS

2 Spring Roll Pastries
1 Egg (beaten)
1 tbsp Chopped Green Onion
2 tsp White Sesames
4 tsp Peanut Powder
1 tsp Chilli Powder
A pinch of Salt

METHOD

Flatten the spring roll pastries, brush beaten egg on them, and then sprinkle chopped green onion, salt and white sesames over. Fold up half of each pastries, add peanut powder and chilli powder on them, and last roll the pastries up.

Prepare a microwave wrap, put the rolls on. Put them in the microwave oven and microwave for 1 minute 30 seconds (850W).

Take them out from the microwave oven and serve.

Satay Deep-Fried Gluten

SERVE

1~2

INGREDIENTS

150g Deep-Fried Gluten (rinsed & cut into chunks)

150g Cucumber (peeled & sliced, to garnish)

2 tbsp Peanut-Satay Paste

2 tbsp Hot Water

METHOD

Blend peanut-satay paste with water well.

Prepare a microwave-safe container, put deep-fried gluten in. Put them in the microwave oven and microwave for 1 minute 30 seconds (850W).

Take them out from the microwave oven. Add 2 tablespoons of blended satay sauce in, and coat the gluten with satay sauce. Put them in the microwave oven and microwave for another 1 minute 30 seconds (850W). Take them out again from the microwave oven.

Prepare a normal plate, put cucumber slices at the bottom, then put gluten on top of cucumber slices, and last spoon the blended satay sauce over gluten and cucumber slices. Serve.

TIPS & NOTES

- The peanut satay paste contains chilli, coconut milk, garlic, satay spices, peanuts, oil, salt, shallot, sugar and vinegar.

Deep-Fried Gluten with Homemade Pandan Kaya

SERVE

1~2

INGREDIENTS

100g Deep-Fried Gluten (rinsed & cut into chunks)

HOMEMADE PANDAN KAYA (MAKE ABOUT 120g)

1 Egg (beaten)
60g Sugar
60ml Coconut Milk
60ml Water
2 drops Pandan Extract

METHOD

To make pandan kaya: put sugar and water in a microwave-safe container. Put them in the microwave oven and microwave for 1 minute (850W).

Take them out from the microwave oven. Whisk until sugar is completely dissolved in water. Add coconut milk in, whisk to blend it well with syrup. Put them in the microwave oven and microwave for 1 minute 30 seconds (850W).

Take them out from the microwave oven. Stir to blend the liquid well. Add beaten egg in. Stir to blend beaten egg well with the liquid until very smooth. Put the mixture in the microwave oven and microwave for 1 minute (850W).

Take them out from the microwave oven. The mixture can be found to be thickened or even set a little. Stir to 'cut' the set mixture smaller. Put them in the microwave oven and microwave for 30 seconds (850W). Repeat this step 3~4 times or until the mixture is set like steamed egg (eg, Japanese chawanmushi/steamed egg custard).

Take the set mixture out from the microwave oven. Put it in a food processor and blend it well until smooth.

To re-heat deep-fried gluten: put them in a microwave-safe container. Then put them in the microwave oven and microwave for 2 minutes 30 seconds (850W).

Take gluten out from the microwave oven. Add pandan kaya in, and stir to coat it on gluten. Serve.

TIPS & NOTES

- Kaya is also known as 'coconut jam', 'srikaya' or 'seri kaya'. It is a very common food spread in Southeast Asia, and it is always served with toasts. Especially in Malaysia and Singapore, kaya toast is a very popular snack there, and served with soft-boiled/half-boiled eggs and coffee or tea.

Stewed King Trumpet Mushroom, Winter Melon and Radish

SERVE

1~2

INGREDIENTS

150g King Trumpet Mushroom (cut into chunks)
150g Winter Melon (peeled & cut into chunks)
150g Chinese Radish (peeled & cut into chunks)
250ml Water
2 Ginger Slices
1 Egg Yolk (beaten)
1 tsp Tapioca Flour
1 tbsp Light Soy Sauce
Pepper

METHOD

Prepare a microwave-safe container, put king trumpet mushroom, radish and ginger slices in, and pour water in. Cover the container with microwave wrap. Put them in the microwave oven and microwave for 5 minutes (850W).

Take them out from the microwave oven and open the microwave wrap. Add winter melon and light soy sauce. Stir to mix all well. Cover the container back with the microwave wrap. Put them in the microwave oven and microwave for another 5 minutes (850W). Take them out from the microwave oven and remove the microwave wrap.

Blend the tapioca flour with 1 tablespoon of water. Add the liquid in the container and blend it well with the soup. Put them in the microwave oven and microwave for 1 minute (850W).

Take them out from the microwave oven. Add egg yolk in and stir to blend it well with the soup. Season with pepper. Serve.

Curried Green Chilli Peppers, Mushrooms and Salted Duck Egg Yolk

SERVE

1~2

INGREDIENTS

150g Canned Sliced Mushrooms (rinsed)
2 Green Chilli Peppers (remove seeds & sliced)
1 Salted Duck Egg Yolk (chopped)
2/3 tbsp Oil
1 tsp Chopped Garlic

SEASONING

2 tbsp Water
1 tsp Sugar
1 tsp Light Soy Sauce
1/2 tsp Indian Curry Powder

METHOD

Prepare a microwave-safe container, put salted duck egg yolk, oil, chopped garlic and all ingredients of seasoning in, and mix them well. Put them in the microwave oven and microwave for 1 minute (850W).

Take them out from the microwave oven. Add mushrooms and green chilli peppers in. Stir to mix all ingredients well. Put them in the microwave oven and microwave for 3 minutes (850W).

Take them out from the microwave oven. Stir once more. Serve.

TIPS & NOTES

- The Indian curry powder used in this recipe contains turmeric, star anise, cinnamon, fennel, ginger, clove and red hot chilli pepper.

Simmered Cabbage, Carrot and Potato in Coconut Milk and Fermented Bean Curd Sauce

SERVE

1~2

INGREDIENTS

200g Cabbage (sliced)
150g Carrot (peeled & cut into chunks)
150g Potato (peeled & cut into chunks)
1/2 tbsp Oil

COCONUT MILK AND FERMENTED BEAN CURD SAUCE

2 cubes Fermented Bean Curds
3 tbsp Coconut Milk
100ml Water

METHOD

Prepare a microwave-safe container, put carrot, potato and oil in, and mix them well. Put them in the microwave oven and microwave for 2 minutes (850W).

Take them out from the microwave oven. Add all other ingredients in. Stir to mix them well. Put them in the microwave oven and microwave for 5 minutes (850W).

Take them out from the microwave oven. Stir one more time. Serve.

Stir-Fried Carrot, Deep-Fried Gluten and Chayote in Peanut-Satay Sauce

SERVE

1~2

INGREDIENTS

150g Carrot (peeled & cut into chunks)
150g Chayote (peeled & cut into chunks)
100g Deep-Fried Gluten (rinsed & cut into chunks)
2 tbsp Peanut-Satay Paste
3 tbsp Water
1 tbsp Oil
1 tsp Sugar

METHOD

Prepare a microwave-safe container, put deep-fried gluten in. Put them in the microwave oven and microwave for 2 minutes 30 seconds (850W). Take them out from the microwave oven.

Prepare another microwave-safe container, put carrot, chayote, 1 tablespoon of water and oil in, and mix them well. Put them in the microwave oven and microwave for 4 minutes (850W).

Take them out from the microwave oven. Add deep-fried gluten, peanut-satay paste, another 2 tablespoons of water and sugar in. Stir to mix all ingredients well. Put them in the microwave oven and microwave for 2 minutes (850W).

Take them out from the microwave oven. Stir one more time. Serve.

TIPS & NOTES

- The peanut satay paste contains chilli, coconut milk, garlic, satay spices, peanuts, oil, salt, shallot, sugar and vinegar.

Stir-Fried Chickpeas, Pineapple and Green Chilli Peppers in Honey Sauce

SERVE

1~2

INGREDIENTS

200g Canned Chickpeas (rinsed)
100g Canned Pineapple Tidbits
2 Green Chilli Peppers (remove seeds & sliced)
3/4 tbsp Oil
1/2 tbsp Honey
1/4 tsp Salt

METHOD

Prepare a microwave-safe container, put chickpeas, green chilli peppers and oil in, and mix them well. Put them in the microwave oven and microwave for 2 minutes 30 seconds (850W).

Take them out from the microwave oven. Add pineapple, honey and salt in. Stir to mix them well with chickpeas and green chilli peppers. Put them in the microwave oven and microwave for another 1 minute (850W).

Take them out from the microwave oven. Stir once more and serve.

Satay Sweet Potato, Onion and Shimeji Mushrooms

SERVE

1~2

INGREDIENTS

150g Orange Sweet Potato (peeled & shredded)
150g Onion (peeled & sliced)
150g Shimeji Mushrooms (rinsed)
1 tbsp Peanut-Satay Paste
1/2 tbsp Oil
Chopped Parsley

METHOD

Prepare a microwave-safe container, put all ingredients in, and stir to mix them well. Put them in the microwave oven and microwave for 4 minutes (850W).

Take them out from the microwave oven. Stir one more time and sprinkle chopped parsley over them. Serve.

TIPS & NOTES

- The peanut satay paste contains chilli, coconut milk, garlic, satay spices, peanuts, oil, salt, shallot, sugar and vinegar.

Curried Apple, Sweet Potato and Potato

SERVE

1~2

INGREDIENTS

150g Orange Sweet Potato (peeled & cut into chunks)
150g Potato (peeled & cut into chunks)
2 Small-Sized Apples (cored & cut into chunks)
3/4 tbsp Oil
1/2 tbsp Indian Curry Powder
1/2 tbsp Light Soy Sauce
1 tsp Chopped Garlic
1/2 tbsp Sugar
120ml Water
120ml Evaporated Milk

METHOD

Prepare a microwave-safe container, put oil, Indian curry powder, light soy sauce, chopped garlic and sugar in, and mix them well. Put them in the microwave oven and microwave for 1 minute (850W).

Take them out from the microwave oven. Add sweet potato and potato in, and pour water in. Stir to mix them well. Put them in the microwave oven and microwave for 4 minutes (850W).

Take them out from the microwave oven. Add apples in, and pour evaporated milk in. Stir to mix all ingredients well. Put them in the microwave oven and microwave for 1 minute (850W).

Take them out from the microwave oven. Stir one more time. Serve.

TIPS & NOTES

- The Indian curry powder used in this recipe contains turmeric, star anise, cinnamon, fennel, ginger, clove and red hot chilli pepper.

SERVE

1~2

INGREDIENTS

300g Hairy Cucumber (peeled & cut into chunks)
2 Eggs (beaten)
1 tbsp Oil
Salt
Pepper

METHOD

Prepare a microwave-safe container, put hairy cucumber and oil in, and mix them well. Put them in the microwave oven and microwave for 3 minutes (850W).

Take them out from the microwave oven. Add beaten eggs in. Stir to mix them well with hairy cucumber. Put them in the microwave oven and microwave for 1 minute 15 seconds (850W).

Take them out from the microwave oven. Season with salt and pepper. Stir one more time and serve.

Satay Bitter Melon and Onion

SERVE

1~2

INGREDIENTS

200g Bitter Melon (remove seeds & cut into chunks)
1/2 Medium-Sized Onion (peeled & sliced)
2 tbsp Peanut-Satay Paste
2 tbsp Hot Water
1 tsp Sugar

METHOD

Blend peanut-satay paste with water well.

Prepare a microwave-safe container, put onion, blended satay sauce and sugar in. Put them in the microwave oven and microwave for 2 minutes (850W).

Take them out from the microwave oven. Add bitter melon in. Stir to mix all ingredients well. Put them in the microwave oven and microwave for another 3 minutes (850W).

Take them out from the microwave oven. Stir one more time. Serve.

TIPS & NOTES

- The peanut satay paste contains chilli, coconut milk, garlic, satay spices, peanuts, oil, salt, shallot, sugar and vinegar.

Potato and Sweet Potato in Portuguese Sauce

SERVE

1~2

INGREDIENTS

250g Potato (peeled & cut into chunks)
250g Orange Sweet Potato (peeled & cut into chunks)
2/3 tbsp Oil
200ml Water

PORTUGESE SAUCE

1/2 tbsp Turmeric Powder
1 tsp Light Soy Sauce
1 tsp Sugar
1 tsp Tapioca Flour
50ml Coconut Milk
50ml Evaporated Milk

METHOD

Blend tapioca flour well with a tablespoonful of water.

Prepare a microwave-safe container, put potato, sweet potato and oil in, and mix them well in. Put them in the microwave oven and microwave for 2 minutes (850W).

Take them out from the microwave oven. Add turmeric powder, light soy sauce and sugar in, and pour water in. Stir to mix them well with potato and sweet potato. Put them in the microwave oven and microwave for 3 minutes (850W).

Take them out from the microwave oven. Add coconut milk and evaporated milk in. Stir to mix it well with the sauce. Put them in the microwave oven and microwave for 2 minutes (850W).

Take them out from the microwave oven. Add tapioca flour mixture in. Stir to mix all ingredients well. Put them in the microwave oven and microwave for 1 minute (850W).

Take them out from the microwave oven. Stir one more time. Serve.

Eggplant and Green Onion Omelette

SERVE

1~2

INGREDIENTS

3 Eggs (beaten)
200g Eggplant (diced)
50g Green Onion (diced)
1 tbsp Oil
Salt
Pepper

METHOD

Prepare a microwave-safe container, put eggplant and oil in, and mix them well. Put them in the microwave oven and microwave for 2 minutes (850W).

Take them out from the microwave oven. Add green onion, salt, pepper and beaten eggs in. Stir to mix all ingredients well. Put them in the microwave oven and microwave for 2 minutes 30 seconds (850W).

Take them out from the microwave oven and serve.

Vegetarian White Sausages

MAKE

6 SAUSAGES

INGREDIENTS

200g Tofu
4 Egg Whites
1.5 tsp Mixed Herbs
1.5 tbsp Margarine (melted)
1.5 tbsp Bread Crumbs
1.5 tbsp Instant Oats
Hot Water
Salt
Pepper

METHOD

Put instant oats in a food processor and blend them into powder form. Then add all other ingredients in and blend them into batter.

Prepare 6 microwave wraps, put the batter on them respectively (about 3 tablespoons each). Wrap the batter into stripe-shape. Knot both ends of the wraps of each roll.

Prepare a microwave-safe container, pour hot water in, and then put the wrapped batter rolls in. Put them in the microwave oven and microwave for 2~4 minutes (850W).

Take them out from the microwave oven. Drain off and unwrap the sausages. Serve with ketchup or mustard or any dipping sauce preferred.

TIPS & NOTES

- The mixed herbs used in this recipe contain peppermint, cinnamon, ginger, lemongrass, and kaffir lime leaves.
- When knotting the ends of the wraps, do not knot too tight and leave a little bit space, as the microwave wraps will be shrunk a little when heating in the microwave oven. Knotting too tight might result having the batter bursting out from the wraps.

- It is recommended to check whether the sausages are cooked or not after microwaving for 2 minutes. Just slightly press the sausages, if they are still undercooked, the pressing area will be concaved and cannot be rebounded back into original shape. Then put them in the microwave oven and microwave for additional 1 minute (850W). Keep checking and microwaving until those sausages are cooked.

Snacks or Desserts

Cucumber Granita

Spring Roll Pastries with Mutabbel

Satay Potato and Sweet Potato

Salt and Pepper Potato

Seaweed, White Sesame and Egg Rolls

Sweet Potato Leaf Rolls

Mission-Fig-and-Raisin Potato

Apple Pie

Cheese Pudding

Green Mungbean and Salted Duck Egg Yolk Pâté

Nutty Tofu

Faux Gras (Vegetarian Foie Gras)

Apple and Cashew Sweet Soup

Pineapple and Sweet Potato Leaves Juice

Winter Melon, Hawthorn and Honey Drink

Cucumber Granita

Seaweed, White Sesame and Egg Rolls

…sion-Fig-and-Raisin Potato

Apple Pie

Green Mungbean and Salted Duck Egg Yolk Pate

[illegible] Tofu

SERVE

1~2

INGREDIENTS

300g Cucumber (peeled)
2 Dried Mission Figs (cut into halves, to garnish)
3 tbsp Water
2 tbsp Sugar
2 tsp Lemon Juice
A pinch of Salt

METHOD

Prepare a microwave-safe container, put water and sugar in. Put them in the microwave oven and microwave for 1 minute 30 seconds (850W).

Take them out from the microwave oven. Whisk to make sure the sugar is completely dissolved in water and become syrup. Cool it in room temperature for several minutes.

Put cucumber in a food processor and blend it well into puree. Add cucumber puree, lemon juice and salt in the microwave-safe container, and blend them well with syrup. Put the mixture in the refrigerator (freezer) until solid.

Take the ice cucumber out from the refrigerator (freezer), use a fork or an ice shaver to scrape it into crystals and spoon them into 2 normal bowls respectively. Put mission figs on top. Serve.

TIPS & NOTES

- Granita is a very good dessert for summer time and it is very easy to make. Besides using cucumber, bitter melon, chayote or other fruits such as guava, mango, pineapple, etc can be used to make granita, if preferred.

Spring Roll Pastries with Mutabbel

SERVE

1~2

INGREDIENTS

200g Eggplant (sectioned)
2 Spring Roll Pastries (cut each into 8 pieces)
2 tbsp Tahini
2 tbsp Lemon Juice
1 tsp Grated Garlic
1 tsp Salt
Chopped Parsley
Olive Oil
Cold Water

METHOD

Prepare a microwave-safe container, put eggplant in. Put the eggplant in the microwave oven and microwave for 6 minutes (850W).

Take the eggplant out from the microwave oven. Pour cold water in to cool down the eggplant. Then drain off, peel and mash the eggplant.

Add tahini, lemon juice, grated garlic and salt in the container with eggplant, and mix them well. Add olive oil and sprinkle chopped parsley over the mixture. The mutabbel is done.

Prepare another microwave-safe container, put spring roll pastries in. Put them in the microwave oven and microwave for 45 seconds (850W).

Take the pastries out from the microwave oven. Serve them with mutabbel.

Satay Potato and Sweet Potato

SERVE

1~2

INGREDIENTS

150g Potato (peeled & cut into chunks)

150g Sweet Potato (peeled & cut into chunks)

1/2 tbsp Peanut-Satay Paste

METHOD

Prepare a baking paper, put potato and sweet potato on. Put them in the microwave oven and microwave for 5 minutes (850W).

Take them out from the microwave oven. Add peanut-satay paste in, and stir to coat the sauce on potato and sweet potato. Put them in the microwave oven and microwave for 2 minutes (850W).

Take them out from the microwave oven and serve.

TIPS & NOTES

- The peanut satay paste contains chilli, coconut milk, garlic, satay spices, peanuts, oil, salt, shallot, sugar and vinegar.

Salt and Pepper Potato

SERVE

1~2

INGREDIENTS

200g Potato (peeled & cut into chunks)
Salt
Black Pepper
Pepper
Grated Cheese

METHOD

Blend salt, black pepper and pepper well.

Coat potato with salt and pepper mixture.

Prepare a baking paper, put potato on. Put them in the microwave oven and microwave for 4 minutes (850W).

Take them out from the microwave oven. Sprinkle grated cheese on the potato. Put them in the microwave oven and microwave for 2 minutes (850W).

Take them out from the microwave oven and serve.

Seaweed, White Sesame and Egg Rolls

SERVE

1~2

INGREDIENTS

2 Spring Roll Pastries
1 Egg (beaten)
2 Japanese Nori (Japanese Edible Seaweeds)
2 tsp White Sesames
A pinch of Salt

METHOD

Flatten the spring roll pastries, put Japanese nori on each of them. Then brush beaten egg on and sprinkle salt and white sesames over, and last roll them up.

Prepare a microwave wrap, put the rolls on. Put them in the microwave oven and microwave for 1 minute 30 seconds (850W).

Take them out from the microwave oven. Cool them in room temperature before serving.

Sweet Potato Leaf Rolls

MAKE

3 Rolls

INGREDIENTS

200g Sweet Potato Leaves
3 Spring Roll Pastries
1/2 tsp Salt
100ml Water

METHOD

Prepare a microwave-safe container, put sweet potato leaves and salt in, and pour water in. Put them in the microwave oven and microwave for 3 minutes (850W).

Take them out from the microwave oven. Put them in a food processor and blend them well. Cool the mixture in room temperature.

Flatten the spring roll pastries, put the mixture over the pastries and roll them respectively.

Prepare 3 baking papers, wrap the rolls in. Put them in the microwave oven and microwave for 4 minutes (850W).

Take them out from the microwave oven. Cool them in room temperature before serving.

SERVE

1~2

INGREDIENTS

250g Potato (peeled)
4 Dried Mission Figs (diced)
1.5 tbsp Raisins
1 tsp Honey
Water

METHOD

Prepare a microwave-safe container, put potato in, and pour water in until 1/3 of potato is covered. Put them in the microwave oven and microwave for 7 minutes (850W). Take the potato out from the microwave oven. Drain it off and mash it.

Blend 1 teaspoon of honey well with 1 tablespoon of water.

Add mission figs, raisins and honey in the container with potato mash, and mix them well. Divide the mixture into 6 portions.

Prepare 6 baking papers, put the portions on respectively. Put them in the microwave oven (arrange them at the outer edge of the glass plate) and microwave for 3 minutes (850W).

Take them out from the microwave oven. Turn them over. Put them back in the microwave oven and microwave for another 3 minutes (850W).

Take them out from the microwave oven. Cool them in room temperature for several minutes before serving.

TIPS & NOTES

- Mission fig is also known as black mission or franciscana.

SERVE

1~2

INGREDIENTS

150g Potato (peeled)
100g Cashew Nuts
75g Tofu
1 Medium-Sized Apple (cored & cut into chunks)
1 tsp Cinnamon Powder
2/3 tsp Salt
Water
Pepper
Red Chilli Powder

METHOD

Prepare a microwave-safe container, put potato in, and pour water in until 1/3 of potato is covered. Put the potato in the microwave oven and microwave for 6 minutes (850W). Take the potato out from the microwave oven, drain it off and cut it into chunks.

Put cashew nuts in a food processor and blend them into powder form. Then add potato, tofu, salt, a pinch of pepper and red chilli powder in, and blend them well. The crust mixture is done.

Prepare another bowl-shaped microwave-safe container, put baking paper on. Put the crust mixture on the baking paper. Use the back of a spoon to smooth the surface of the crust.

Put apple and cinnamon powder in a food processor and blend them well. Pour the apple mixture onto the crust, and use the back of a spoon to smooth the surface of apple mixture. Put them in the microwave oven and microwave for 8 minutes (850W).

Take them out from the microwave oven and cool it in room temperature for several minutes. Serve.

TIPS & NOTES

- Pepper and Red Chilli Powder are optional to add into the crust mixture, but from my very own point of view, eating the pie with the mixture of sweet and a little spicy is tasty.

MAKE

2 Puddings

INGREDIENTS

120g Egg Tofu
40g Instant Oats
40g Cheddar Cheese
1/3 Medium-Sized Onion (peeled & diced)
Salt
Pepper
Black Sesames

METHOD

Put instant oats in a food processor and blend them into powder form.

Add egg tofu, cheddar cheese, onion, salt and pepper in the food processor and blend them together with oats into batter form.

Prepare 2 microwave-safe container, pour the mixture in respectively. Sprinkle some black sesames on the top of each of them. Cover the containers with 2 baking papers respectively. Put them in the microwave oven and microwave for 4 minutes (850W).

Take them out from the microwave oven and remove the baking papers. Serve.

SERVE

1~2

INGREDIENTS

2 Salted Duck Egg Yolk (cut into halves)
4 tbsp Dried Dehulled Green Mungbeans
1/3 tsp Sugar
1/4 tsp Salt
Water

METHOD

Prepare a normal container, put dried dehulled green mungbeans in, and pour water in until the green mungbeans are fully covered. Soak green mungbeans in water for 3~4 hours or until those beans are getting larger in size. Then drain off and rinse them.

Prepare a microwave-safe container, put green mungbeans, 1.5 salted duck egg yolk, sugar and salt in, and pour water in until all ingredients are covered. Put them in the microwave oven, microwave for 8 minutes (850W) and stay put in the microwave oven for 4 minutes.

Keep them in the microwave oven and microwave for another 8 minutes (850W).

Take them out from the microwave oven and drain off. Put them in a food processor and blend them well into puree. Divide the green mungbean puree into 12 small portions.

Prepare a normal plate and 2 teaspoons. Use the teaspoons to shape the green mungbean puree like ovals, and put them on the plate.

Prepare another microwave-safe container, put the left 1/2 salted duck egg yolk in, and pour water in until it is covered. Put the duck egg yolk in the microwave oven and microwave for 5 minutes (850W).

Take the duck egg yolk out from the microwave oven and drain off. Put it in the food processor and blend it into flakes. Sprinkle the duck egg yolk flakes over green mungbean puree. Serve.

TIPS & NOTES

- Mung bean is also called 'mungbean', 'mung', 'green gram', or 'golden gram'. It is also known as 'mongo', 'moong', 'moog' (whole bean) or 'moog dal' (split bean) in India; 'mung eta' in Sri Lanka; 'ludou' in China; 'dau xanh' in Vietnam; and 'kacang hijau' or 'katjang idju' in Indonesia. Green mung beans and red mung beans are commonly used in Chinese cuisine, such as making the dessert 'green bean soup' and 'red bean soup'.

SERVE

1~2

INGREDIENTS

100g Tofu
40g Salted Mixed Nuts
2 tsp Black and White Sesames
1/3 tsp Salt
50ml Water

METHOD

Put salted mixed nuts and water in a food processor and blend them well. Add tofu and salt in, and continue to blend until very smooth. Then add black and white sesames in, and mix them well with the nutty tofu mixture.

Prepare a microwave-safe container, pour the nutty tofu mixture in. Put them in the microwave oven and microwave for 3 minutes (850W).

Take them out from the microwave oven. Stir to blend the mixture well.

Chill it in the refrigerator and slice it before serving.

TIPS & NOTES

- Salted Mixed Nuts contain almonds, Brazil nuts, cashew nuts, hazelnuts, macadamia nuts, peanuts and pecans.
- Re-heat the nutty tofu by microwaving it for 1 minute 30 seconds (850W) after chilling in the refrigerator, if serving warm is preferred.

Faux Gras (Vegetarian Foie Gras)

SERVE

1~2

INGREDIENTS

100g Canned Chickpeas (rinsed)
50g Canned Mushrooms (rinsed)
50g Onion (peeled & sliced)
4 tbsp Margarine
1 tbsp Olive Oil
1/2 tsp Lime Juice
1/4 tsp Salt
30ml Red Wine
Pepper

METHOD

Prepare a microwave-safe container, put onion, olive oil and 2 tablespoons of margarine in. Stir to mix them well. Put them in the microwave oven and microwave for 3 minutes (850W).

Take them out from the microwave oven. Add chickpeas, mushrooms and red wine in. Stir to mix them well with onion. Put them in the microwave oven and microwave for another 5 minutes (850W).

Take them out from the microwave oven. Cool them in room temperature. Then put them in a food processor. Add lime juice, salt and pepper in the food processor as well, and blend them well until becoming smooth puree.

Prepare another microwave-safe container, put 2 tablespoons of margarine in. Put the margarine in the microwave oven and microwave for 20 seconds (850W). Take the margarine out from the microwave oven. Whisk it to make sure the margarine is completely melted.

Prepare a normal container, pour the chickpea puree in, and then pour melted margarine over the puree. Chill them in the refrigerator until set. Serve with breads or crackers if preferred.

Apple and Cashew Sweet Soup

SERVE

1~2

INGREDIENTS

100g Apple (cored & cut into chunks)
20g Roasted Cashew Nuts
300ml Water
Honey

METHOD

Put apple, roasted cashew nuts and water in a food processor and blend them well.

Prepare a microwave-safe container, pour apple and roasted cashew nuts mixture in. Put them in the microwave oven and microwave for 8 minutes (850W).

Take them out from the microwave oven. Season with honey, and stir to mix the soup well. Serve.

Pineapple and Sweet Potato Leaves Juice

SERVE

1~2

INGREDIENTS

100g Canned Pineapple Tidbits

50g Sweet Potato Leaves

400ml Water

Sugar

METHOD

Prepare a microwave-safe container, put sweet potato leaves in, and pour water in. Put them in the microwave oven and microwave for 3 minutes (850W).

Take them out from the microwave oven. Add sugar in, and stir to melt sugar completely. Then cool them in room temperature.

Put pineapple and sweet potato leaves (with liquid) in a food processor and blend them into juice.

Chill the juice in the refrigerator before serving.

Winter Melon, Hawthorn and Honey Drink

SERVE

1~2

INGREDIENTS

200g Winter Melon (peeled & diced)
60g (4 rolls) Haw Flakes
600ml Water
Honey

METHOD

Prepare a microwave-safe container, put winter melon and haw flakes in, and pour water in. Cover the container with microwave wrap. Put them in the microwave oven, microwave for 8 minutes (850W) and stay put in the microwave oven for 4 minutes.

Keep them in the microwave oven. Microwave them for 8 minutes (850W) and stay put in the microwave oven for 4 minutes. Repeat this step twice.

Take them out from the microwave oven. Pour the liquid in a food processor and blend it well.

Cool it in refrigerator. Add honey in before serving.

TIPS & NOTES

- Haw Flakes are kind of sweets that made from Chinese hawthorn, and packed in rolls.

Wancy Ganst's

Microwave Cooking Series

Microwave Cooking: Easy & Simple Asian & Fusion Recipes

Available at:

https://www.createspace.com/3550731

Microwave Cooking 2: Vegetarian Recipes

Available at:

https://www.createspace.com/3558580

Microwave Cooking 3: Another Vegetarian Recipes

Available at:

https://www.createspace.com/3630470

Microwave Cooking 4: Meat?-Not-Meat! Recipes

Available at:

https://www.createspace.com/3630471

Microwave Cooking 5: The Return of Vegetarian Recipes

Available at:

https://www.createspace.com/3630473

Wancy Ganst's

Microwave Cooking Series

Microwave Cooking 6: Konnyaku Recipes

Available at:

https://www.createspace.com/3641801

Microwave Cooking 7: Vegetarian Recipes Number Four

Available at:

https://www.createspace.com/3660356

Microwave Cooking 8: More Meat?-Not-Meat! Recipes

Available at:

https://www.createspace.com/3660361

Microwave Cooking 9: The Fifth Vegetarian Cookbook

Available at:

https://www.createspace.com/3680503

Microwave Cooking 10: Keep On Vegetarian Recipes

Available at:

https://www.createspace.com/3685289

Wancy Ganst's

Microwave Cooking Series

Microwave Cooking 11: Meat?-Not-Meat! Recipes More More More

Available at:

https://www.createspace.com/3699575

Microwave Cooking 12: Vegetarian Recipes Continue…

Available at:

https://www.createspace.com/3717196

Wancy Ganst's Other Book

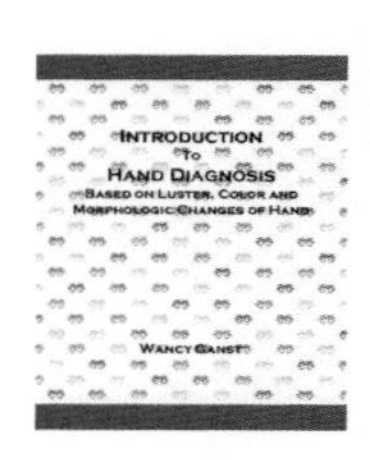

Introduction to Hand Diagnosis

Based on Luster, Color and Morphologic Changes of Hand

Available at:

https://www.createspace.com/3542692

Printed in Great Britain
by Amazon